BIONIC BEASTS

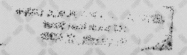

BIONIC BEASTS

Saving Animal Lives with Artificial Flippers, Legs, and Beaks

JOLENE GUTIÉRREZ

M MILLBROOK PRESS · MINNEAPOLIS

In memory of my dad and in honor of my mom, who fostered my love of animals and nature. Thank you for telling me to go outside to play and letting me surround myself with animals.

Millbrook Press™
An imprint of Lerner Publishing Group, Inc.
241 First Avenue North
Minneapolis, MN 55401 USA

For reading levels and more information, look up this title at www.lernerbooks.com.

Designed by Viet Chu.
Main body text set in Frutiger LT Std. Typeface provided by Adobe Systems.

Library of Congress Cataloging-in-Publication Data

Names: Gutiérrez, Jolene, author.
Title: Bionic beasts : saving animal lives with artificial flippers, legs, and beaks / Jolene Gutiérrez.
Description: Minneapolis : Millbrook Press, [2021] | Includes bibliographical references and index. | Audience: Ages 9–14 | Audience: Grades 4–6 | Summary: "Using innovative designs and technology such as 3-D printing, humans are helping animals in need. Discover the amazing true stories of five animals that have survived thanks to their prosthetic body parts" —Provided by publisher.
Identifiers: LCCN 2019050146 (print) | LCCN 2019050147 (ebook) | ISBN 9781541589407 (library binding) | ISBN 9781728401492 (ebook)
Subjects: LCSH: Veterinary surgery—Juvenile literature. | Prosthesis—Juvenile literature. | Bionics—Juvenile literature. | Medical technology—Juvenile literature.
Classification: LCC SF911 .G88 2021 (print) | LCC SF911 (ebook) | DDC 636.089/7—dc23

LC record available at https://lccn.loc.gov/2019050146
LC ebook record available at https://lccn.loc.gov/2019050147

Manufactured in the United States of America
1-47474-48030-2/28/2020

CONTENTS

INTRODUCTION

NOT LONG AGO, A BIRD WITHOUT A BEAK MIGHT HAVE STARVED TO DEATH.
An elephant without a foot would have hobbled painfully, permanently damaging her spine and remaining legs. Now animals like these are becoming bionic beasts, animals who have artificial body parts that help them move or function.

A sea turtle might lose a flipper due to an encounter with a predator or by becoming tangled in fishing line.

Thanks to sophisticated design software and 3-D printers, we have new ways to help injured animals.

Using innovative designs and technology such as 3-D printing, humans can help animals in need. People around the globe—including students like you—are making custom prostheses, replacement bionic body parts that allow animals to move, eat, and live their best lives.

In this book, you'll meet five animals from the United States, India, Brazil, and Canada and learn how humans have helped them by using new technologies, science, and innovation. Are you ready to find out what happens to a goose with no beak or a dog without a leg? Is it possible for a heavy animal like an elephant or a pig to walk on only three legs? Can a turtle with one flipper survive in the ocean? Read on to find out!

CHAPTER 1

LOLA'S NEW FLIPPER

A Kemp's Ridley Sea Turtle's Story

Lola swims in her habitat at the Key West Aquarium in Key West, Florida.

On July 27, 2002, a female Kemp's ridley sea turtle weighing less than 1 ounce (28 g) was found on Mustang Island, Texas. The hatchling was in pain and unable to swim. She had washed up on the beach and was partially buried in sand. A fish had bitten off part of her right front flipper and injured her spine and intestines. She was so weak that she couldn't pull herself from the sand.

Tony Amos, wildlife rehabilitator and director of the Animal Rehabilitation Keep, or ARK, welcomed the little turtle to their center in Port Aransas, Texas. Staff estimated she was a few weeks old and gave her an identification number, LK-02-112. Even though turtle LK-02-112 was injured, staff at ARK hoped to release her back into the ocean once she healed. They tagged her with a tiny tracking device the size of a grain of rice.

Over the next eleven months, the turtle grew larger and stronger and learned to swim with her injured flipper. Then, on June 3, 2003, ARK staff sailed 8 miles (13 km) out into the Gulf of Mexico to set her free.

ABOUT KEMP'S RIDLEY SEA TURTLES

Kemp's ridley sea turtles are critically endangered. In fact, they're the most endangered sea turtle in the world! These turtles are named after Richard Kemp, a fisherman from Florida who discovered and studied them in the late 1800s.

Most Kemp's ridleys live in the Gulf of Mexico. They are one of the smallest types of sea turtles, living approximately fifty years, weighing an average of 75 to 100 pounds (34 to 45 kg) and growing to about 24 inches (61 cm) long. Kemp's ridleys have become endangered due in large part to threats like pollution, the destruction of their nesting areas, and poachers hunting them for their eggs, meat, and shells.

The rare Kemp's ridley sea turtles are an olive-green color. The color helps them blend in with the sandy bottoms of shallow waters.

The nesting habits of Kemp's ridleys put them at additional risk. Scientists hypothesize that sea turtles use Earth's magnetic fields and a heightened sense of smell to practice natal homing, returning to the beach they hatched from. This means that Kemp's ridleys return to the same beaches, year after year. Kemp's ridleys are also the only sea turtles that regularly lay their eggs during the day. Both of these behaviors make their nests easier for poachers to find. People who steal the eggs take them to cities where they are sold to restaurants and are eaten as a delicacy. Kemp's ridleys are protected by various countries and are internationally listed as critically endangered, though, so hunting them and disturbing their nesting sites is illegal. Poachers may be required to pay fines and even sentenced to jail for their crimes.

When a sea turtle eats a plastic bag, the trash can suffocate the turtle or become stuck in the its digestive tract, causing pain and even death.

The plastic trash in our oceans poses another danger for Kemp's ridleys and other sea turtles. Sea turtles like to eat jellyfish, and they may mistake things like plastic bags and plastic fishing lines or nets as jellyfish. When the turtles try to eat the trash, they can suffocate or experience other serious injuries.

Unfortunately, the next day, a mother and her children found turtle LK-02-112 as they were exploring the beach. Fishing line was wrapped so tightly around what remained of the little turtle's right front flipper that most of the flipper eventually had to be amputated.

LK-02-112 was sent to the Texas State Aquarium in Corpus Christi, where staff gave her a name, Lola. Lola now weighed about 8 pounds (3.6 kg), but she spent her days restlessly swimming in small circles, bumping against the side of the tank. Her intact left flipper was stronger than her residual right flipper, so she couldn't swim in a straight line. Because of her injuries, aquarium staff decided she'd need to live in a rescue center or aquarium for the rest of her life.

Iok Wong (*left*) and Samantha Varela (*second from left*) work with Douglas Mader (*second from right*) and Greg Gerwin (*right*) to prepare Lola for her prosthesis.

On April 12, 2008, the Key West Aquarium (KWAQ) in Florida offered a home to Lola. At this point, she weighed 55 pounds (25 kg), but even though she was growing, Lola didn't seem happy.

Greg Gerwin, former curator at KWAQ, said, "With her flipper missing, Lola would only swim in circles, which caused her a lot of discomfort during feeding. She would pretty much just stay at the bottom, not moving around that much. It's actually kind of sad to watch, because these turtles out in the ocean swim freely, and they have the ability to move so gracefully. She didn't."

Then, Douglas Mader, the veterinarian at KWAQ, got an email message from college students at Worcester Polytechnic Institute (WPI). Vivian Liang, Samantha Varela, and Iok Wong were working on a capstone design project and wanted to create a replacement flipper for a sea turtle amputee.

Gerwin and Mader sent photographs, measurements, dimensions, and x-rays to the students. Wong noted, "Her swimming capabilities are hindered due to the amputation. She has trouble balancing, turning, and avoiding collisions with her tank. Lola's swimming patterns likely cause excess stress on her remaining healthy limbs. Lola is a very young sea turtle, but with her amputation stressing her remaining limbs, her life expectancy was shortened."

The WPI students worked to create a prosthetic flipper for Lola. Liang, Varela, and Wong researched sea turtle anatomy and learned about the motions turtle flippers make while swimming. They planned to create a biomimetic flipper that would fit Lola specifically and mimic the way her healthy flipper moved. Turtle flipper movements in the water are much like bird wing movements in the air, so the team used a wind tunnel to test the performance of miniature flipper prototypes.

Once they'd found a flipper shape that performed the way they wanted it to in the wind tunnel, the students 3-D printed a life-size hard plastic flipper template. The team used that flipper to make a negative mold by pouring silicone around the flipper and letting it cure, then removing the plastic flipper from inside the now-hardened silicone mold. They used this "Popsicle-type" mold and poured in a flexible silicone that would become Lola's new flipper.

Varela said, "We tried to use a type of silicone that was just right in flexibility so that it would be able to push the water out of the way during swimming while bending to the water at the same time, to mimic the sea turtle's natural 'wing-like/flying in water' movement."

In 2016, Varela and Wong traveled to Florida to fit Lola with the prosthesis. They affixed the silicone flipper to a socket they'd designed to surround and protect Lola's residual flipper and then attached the entire device to Lola with Velcro straps that were riveted onto the socket.

UPDATED FLIPPER!

After Varela, Wong, and Liang completed their project and graduated from college, a second WPI student team decided to help improve the fit of Lola's flipper so she wouldn't develop pressure sores. They brainstormed ways to attach the flipper, including a glove design and a jacket and harness design. The team hoped the prosthesis they created could be used for other turtles, including Lola's tankmate, Rocky, a green sea turtle who lost his right flipper after being hit by a boat.

The students reached out to the Hanger Clinic and prosthetist Kevin Carroll. In 2007 Carroll had created a prosthetic tail for Winter, a dolphin who lost her tail after getting caught in a crab trap. Carroll thought that some of his patented materials might help cushion Lola and Rocky's residual flippers. After creating prosthetic flippers for the turtles, Carroll fitted them with their new prostheses and released them back into their tank. This was Rocky's first time with a prosthesis, but even so, Carroll said, "Lola and Rocky took to their new flippers in no time!"

Kemp's ridley sea turtles are known for thrashing their flippers and biting humans who try to interact with them. According to curator Genya Yerkes, Lola is usually "notoriously bitey," but when the WPI students fitted her new flipper on her, she let them strap the prosthesis on without ever trying to bite them.

Then they released Lola into the water. Would Lola's right shoulder muscle be strong enough to move the flipper blade through the water? Yes!

"She was a fast learner!" Varela said. The biomimetic design of the prosthesis may also have helped Lola learn to use the flipper. According to Varela, "This was a prosthetic [flipper]—one of the very first of its kind—that attempted to imitate the sea turtle's natural swimming locomotion called the powerstroke."

Soon Lola was wearing her prosthetic flipper all day. She seemed to enjoy the speed her new flipper gave her, only resting when staff took the prosthesis off at night.

Because of the injuries Lola sustained after being tangled in fishing line, she can never be released into the wild. Instead, KWAQ staff use Lola and her story to help teach others about the threats sea turtles face and how we can help.

Watching the sea turtle dive and swim, Gerwin said, "Now, with her prosthetic [flipper], we have hope for Lola."

Lola power stroking with her prosthetic flipper

FLOPPY FLIPPERS: LOLA

The WPI students who designed Lola's prosthesis had to experiment to find the right consistency of the silicone they used for her flipper. The following recipes use dessert gels rather than silicone. Test these recipes, and then experiment with them. What happens if you add less water? What happens if you add more gelatin or agar-agar? What happens if you tilt the pan and the gel is thinner on one side than the other? Try to cut flipper shapes out of your gel, and test how they might function in the water. Does your gel formula need to be firmer? More flexible? How can you change it? These are some of the questions WPI students asked themselves as they created Lola's flipper.

SUPPLIES NEEDED

- **1 cup boiling water**
- **3 ounce package of gelatin dessert, such as Jell-O, any flavor**
- **9 × 13-inch casserole dish**

1. Get an adult's help to bring the water to a boil.
2. Pour the package of gelatin powder into your casserole dish, and once the water is boiling, add it to the casserole dish and stir until the gelatin is completely dissolved.
3. Refrigerate until set, approximately 4 hours.

ALTERNATE RECIPE

- **1 cup boiling water**
- **3 ounce package of Jell-O gelatin, any flavor**
- **¼ ounce envelope Knox Gelatine unflavored gelatin**
- **9 × 13-inch casserole dish**

Follow the instructions from above. This version will be firmer than the first version.

VEGETARIAN/VEGAN RECIPE

- **3 teaspoons agar-agar powder**
- **½ cup water**
- **½ cup fruit juice**
- **⅛ cup sugar (optional)**
- **9 × 13-inch casserole dish**

1. Mix all ingredients in a saucepan, and bring to a boil, stirring frequently.
2. Boil for two minutes, still stirring, before pouring into a casserole dish.
3. Refrigerate until set. Note: this version won't be quite as flexible as the gelatin versions.

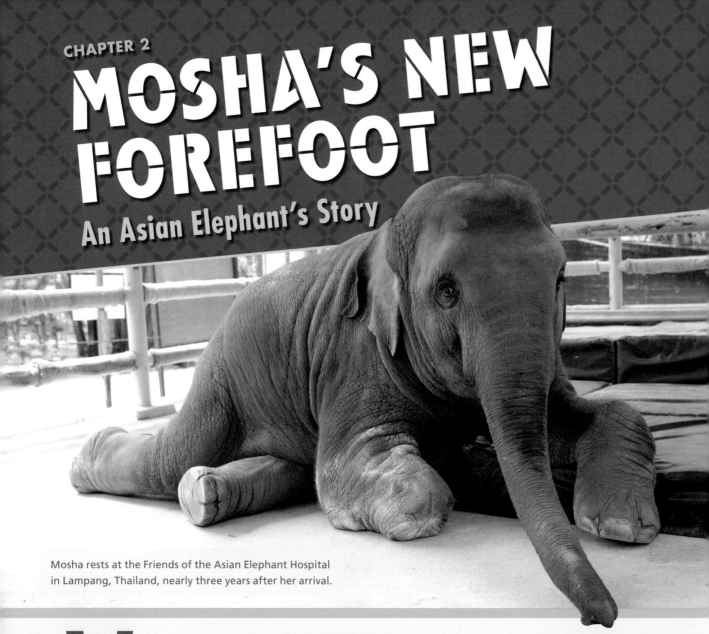

CHAPTER 2

MOSHA'S NEW FOREFOOT

An Asian Elephant's Story

Mosha rests at the Friends of the Asian Elephant Hospital in Lampang, Thailand, nearly three years after her arrival.

Wood is an important resource in the countries of Thailand and Myanmar (also called Burma). Due to logging bans in Thailand, Thai loggers often travel to Myanmar to cut down trees. They cross the border with Asian elephants that will help harvest and transport heavy logs. Decades-long civil wars in Myanmar have created some dangerous conditions for the elephants and their handlers, though. Soldiers have buried explosive land mines as a way of trying to protect their property from other invading groups.

On June 9, 2006, near the border of Thailand and Myanmar, a female elephant and her seven-month-old baby were moving logs. When the baby elephant stepped on a buried land mine, the bomb exploded. The mother elephant was fine, but the baby was terribly injured, having lost her right front foot.

The elephants' owner immediately knew they needed to go to the Friends of the Asian Elephant (FAE) Hospital, the world's first elephant hospital. The facility was located in northwestern Thailand, a journey that could take days, but there was no other choice. The owner loaded the baby and her mother into a truck and drove two days to the FAE Hospital. They arrived in the middle of the night, and the founder of the hospital, Soraida Salwala, met them. "When they opened the back of the truck, two elephants were standing there. One big one, and this tiny creature stood there with two bright eyes, still wide open, from fear, from pain. And it was after midnight. That was why I named her Mosha. Because in Karen language, it means the stars."

Salwala had seen injuries like this before. Each year, hundreds of innocent humans and animals are injured or even killed by hidden land mines. If the owners of injured elephants are able to get them to the FAE Hospital, Salwala's staff cares for the elephants, free of charge.

Salwala and FAE employees put medication and antibiotics into fruit jam to feed to the baby elephant rather than giving injections that might cause more pain and stress. Even though they fed Mosha jam-medication for a little over a month, her wound became infected. The small elephant nearly died, but one of the supporters of the hospital sent medicinal herbs to help fight the infection. Over the next few months, Mosha's wound began to heal and slowly began to close.

ASIAN ELEPHANT FACTS

Asian elephants (*pictured below*) are a bit smaller than African elephants. A full-grown Asian elephant generally weighs between 6,000 and 12,000 pounds (2,722 and 5,443 kg) and stands from 6 to 10 feet (1.8 to 3 m) tall at the shoulders. Asian elephants are found throughout South and Southeast Asia. There are three subspecies of Asian elephants: Sri Lankan, Sumatran, and Indian, which is the subspecies found in Thailand. All the Asian elephant subspecies are critically endangered.

Fewer elephants mean problems for Asian forests because elephants are crucial to the landscape. As they eat and move through a forest, they spread seeds and clear overgrown plants. If they can't find water, they'll dig to bring it to the surface, providing water for themselves and other animals. Elephants are the largest land mammals, and they are extremely smart. They are some of the only animals who recognize themselves in a mirror, and they can communicate over long distances with rumbling sounds that are picked up through the footpads of other elephants.

As Mosha's injury healed, Salwala and her staff installed a metal railing in Mosha's enclosure that Mosha could lean on for support. Even so, Mosha's remaining front leg was bowing and becoming curved because it was carrying too much weight. When elephants walk, the majority of their weight is held by the front of their body. Because Mosha was missing her right forefoot, two-thirds of her weight was being supported by her front left leg. When Mosha is full grown, she will weigh over 6,000 pounds (2,722 kg), which means more than 4,000 pounds (1,814 kg) will be

Soraida Salwala, founder of the Friends of the Asian Elephant Hospital, near Motala and her caregiver, Samwong Waronviriya

supported by her remaining front leg. Mosha hobbled on three legs with her trunk in the air, trying to balance herself. Even though she wasn't yet full grown, the weight Mosha's left foreleg was being forced to support was already damaging her cartilage and twisting her leg and spine.

MOTALA, ANOTHER FAE ELEPHANT WITH A PROSTHESIS

Mosha is not the only elephant at FAE who has lost a leg to a land mine. Motala was already at the Friends of the Asian Elephant Hospital when Mosha arrived. Motala was transported to FAE in 1999 after stepping on a land mine in the forests of Myanmar. Orthopedist Therdchai Jivacate wanted to create a prosthetic leg for Motala, but he couldn't fit her with one until her injuries were healed, a process that took approximately ten years. Motala also weighed more than Mosha, so Jivacate wasn't certain he could create a leg that would hold all of Motala's weight. After Mosha was successfully fitted with a prosthetic leg, though, Jivacate felt he had the knowledge and skills to help Motala. Jivacate and Salwala started work on a device for Motala in 2009. Because Motala is older and her leg is more tender than Mosha's, Motala hasn't adapted to her new leg as quickly as Mosha. Even so, the prosthesis takes much of the strain off Motala's spine and remaining foreleg, and Motala builds her strength by walking outside and wading in a physical therapy pond.

By the time Mosha was two years old, Therdchai Jivacate, a renowned orthopedist for humans, was working with his team to design a prosthesis for the young elephant. This would be the first prosthetic leg and foot ever created for an elephant. Jivacate had been an orthopedist and surgeon for years, and in 1992, he founded the Prostheses Foundation to provide free prostheses to humans. In that time, he has created more than twenty thousand prosthetic legs for patients, including dogs, cats, and birds as well as humans.

One of Jivacate's challenges was using materials that would be strong enough to withstand thousands of pounds of weight while providing enough cushioning that the device wouldn't hurt Mosha's tender residual limb.

After making molds of Mosha's leg, Jivacate created a 33-pound (15 kg) prosthesis from a sturdy polypropylene thermoplastic, similar to the plastic liners used in the beds of pickup trucks. He lined and cushioned the sleeve and supported the bottom with a steel pipe and footplate. The very bottom of the prosthesis was made from the same type of rubber used in shock absorbers for cars.

Before putting on the prosthesis, Mosha's residual limb was covered in baby powder and a large nylon sock was stretched over the limb to protect it from pressure wounds. The prosthesis slipped over the nylon stocking like a boot. Strong straps had been riveted onto the prosthetic leg, and these straps could be tightened to help hold the prosthesis on Mosha's leg. As she got used to the leg, Mosha explored it with her trunk and even tried to remove it, but it was securely attached. Over the course of the next twelve hours, Mosha learned to walk on her new leg. Jivacate and his team made adjustments to the prosthesis until Mosha was walking smoothly.

As Mosha grew, Jivacate continued to create new devices. During her first year of wearing prostheses, Mosha outgrew three prosthetic legs. With each iteration, Jivacate evaluated and modified the design and materials. He said, "Every time we fix it, we improve it. This one's sturdy, stronger. This is not in the textbook. Sometimes [we have

Therdchai Jivacate in the Chiang Mai University Prosthetics Lab in Chiang Mai, Thailand. Jivacate designs both human and elephant prostheses in this lab.

Mosha walks with her mahout, or caregiver, Palahdee Sujaritsuchada.

to figure it out through] trial and error." Mosha's current leg is supported by multiple steel pipes and has a joint that bends.

Mosha has outgrown thirteen prostheses, and because she continues to grow, she'll need a new leg every six months or so. The Friends of the Asian Elephant Hospital has added their own factory that will help make devices for Mosha and other elephants.

Because Mosha's mother wasn't hurt in the explosion that injured Mosha, her owner took her back and continued logging work in the forest. Mosha's injuries mean she can't work as a logging elephant, so she will spend the rest of her life at the Friends of the Asian Elephant Hospital, socializing with other elephants and her human caregiver, Palahdee Sujaritsuchada.

With her new jointed prosthesis, Mosha loves traveling around the Friends of the Asian Elephant sanctuary. Before Mosha had this leg, she was unable to walk on some of the uneven ground, but now, she's able to play and explore. Each evening, her leg is removed so she will rest, but if Sujaritsuchada is delayed in the morning, Mosha cries and calls for her prosthetic leg.

According to Jivacate, "I think it means so much for her. She can lead a normal life as she should be."

GIVE ELEPHANTS A HAND: MOSHA

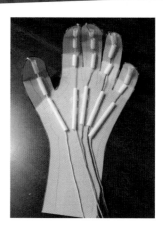

Just as Jivacate has to think about how Mosha's leg will bend, you can think about how fingers bend by building your own robotic hand.

SUPPLIES NEEDED

- **pencil**
- **1 piece of cardstock or cardboard**
- **scissors**
- **tape**
- **3 to 5 compostable drinking straws or paper straws**
- **embroidery thread or yarn of various colors (try a different color for each finger!)**
- **large plastic needle (optional)**

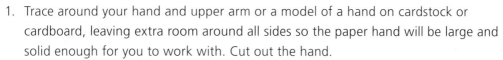

1. Trace around your hand and upper arm or a model of a hand on cardstock or cardboard, leaving extra room around all sides so the paper hand will be large and solid enough for you to work with. Cut out the hand.

2. Flip your paper over so the opposite side from what you drew on is faceup. Look at your own hand. Do you see your finger joints? These are the parts that are able to bend. Using your hand as a model, mark lines on your paper hand at the areas where the joints should bend. Fold your paper fingers and thumbs at these lines.

3. You will use the straws to represent bones. Cut your compostable straws into smaller pieces of approximately ½ inch (1.3 cm) for the phalanges or finger bones and 2 inches (5 cm) long for the metacarpal bones on the palm area of the hand. Tape the "bones" onto the palm side of the hand, leaving gaps between the straws in order to thread the yarn through. Use enough tape to hold the straws securely, but try not to smash the straws.

4. The thread or yarn represents tendons, tissues that attach muscles to bones. Take one strand of yarn and place it over the tip of one of the paper fingers, taping it on the back of the hand. Thread the yarn down through the straws, leaving it a bit longer than the paper wrist. After you've added yarn for each finger, gather the yarn at the wrist and practice moving your robotic hand's fingers. You can tie loops at the end of your yarn to make manipulating the fingers easier.

5. As you bend the fingers, think about all the parts that need to work properly to create movement in a hand or a leg. How do you think this design is similar to Mosha's leg prosthesis? How is it different? What improvements might you make to this design?

CHAPTER 3

CASSIDY'S NEW LEG

A German Shepherd's Story

Cassidy with his best friend, Bella (*left*), at the Posovskys' home near New York City, New York.

In 2005, Stephen Posovsky saw a report about a sick, skinny, three-legged dog on the local television news. The German shepherd mix had been found wandering the streets of the Bronx, a borough of New York City. He was missing half his hair and was approximately 30 pounds (14 kg) underweight. Shelter staff took the dog in and named him Cassidy.

Posovsky was passionate about rescuing animals that might need extra care and support, and he wanted to help Cassidy. He drove from his home just outside of New York City to visit the shelter and meet the dog.

As soon as Posovsky met Cassidy, he wanted the dog to join his family, but shelter workers knew that nursing Cassidy back to health would require much time, effort, and money. They weren't ready to send the dog home with just anyone. Posovsky finally convinced the workers to let him adopt Cassidy, explaining that he and his wife had rescued many animals in the past. Because he had volunteered in shelters before, Posovsky had seen that most people wanted to rescue puppies. He knew that a full-grown patchy-haired dog who was struggling to walk would be difficult for the shelter to place in a forever home. Posovsky also knew the shelter might have to euthanize Cassidy if he wasn't placed in a home soon because there wasn't space for all the dogs coming in. "I wanted to guarantee I'd save a life," Posovsky said.

Living with the Posovskys, Cassidy gained weight and his hair started growing back. Still, the young, energetic dog wasn't able to run and jump. When the Posovskys moved to their home in Florida, Cassidy loved visiting the beach but struggled to walk in the sand. His back leg carried much of his weight and he moved with a hunched posture. He wasn't able to play and enjoy his time outside as the Posovskys had hoped. Susan Posovsky said, "We could see from the way he was walking that it was very difficult for him."

Supporting his weight on only three legs could cause damage to Cassidy's spine and joints. Posovsky worried that Cassidy might injure his other legs, so he started researching options that could help his dog. Posovsky learned that North Carolina State University (NCSU) College of Veterinary Medicine was doing innovative work in fitting animals with prostheses, so they made an appointment with Denis Marcellin-Little, professor of orthopedic surgery, and traveled approximately 500 miles (805 km) to meet him.

Marcellin-Little examined Cassidy and designed a removable prosthetic leg for the dog. Over the course of a year, Marcellin-Little and the Posovskys fitted Cassidy with various types of prostheses. Cassidy kicked each

THE NUTS AND BOLTS OF OSSEOINTEGRATION

When Marcellin-Little performs an osseointegration surgery, his team makes a customized implant of textured titanium. After surgery, the patient's bone will start to grow around the metal. Because the metal is rough instead of smooth, the bone will merge more easily with the metal implant. Before their patient ever arrives, the team has created the implant, also called a free-form implant, that should fit perfectly into the animal's bone. Using 3-D-printed bones created from the CT scan data, Marcellin-Little and his team practice and rehearse the surgery beforehand to be sure that the endoprosthesis is an exact fit.

Once the patient arrives, the surgical procedure begins. The team pushes the implant firmly into or around the bone. The endoprosthesis is often secured with screws or bolts to keep it in place while the bone grows into it. Once the bone grows into the implant, also known as ingrowth, the endoprosthesis should be stable and strong.

Cassidy's residual limb is covered by a rubber cap Posovsky invented to protect the implant site after the endoprosthesis surgery.

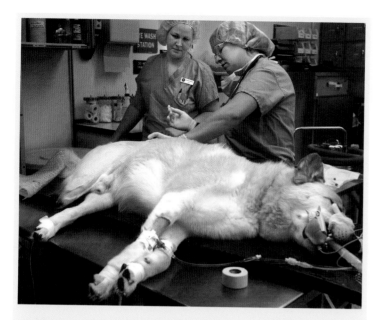

Anesthetists at North Carolina's State University College of Veterinary Medicine in Raleigh, North Carolina, prepare Cassidy for his osseointegration surgery.

prosthesis off as soon as it was attached to his body.

Even though Cassidy rejected the prostheses, he continued to struggle with mobility. At that point, Marcellin-Little and the Posovskys discussed the possibility of a permanent osseointegrated prosthesis, or endoprosthesis. This is a metal prosthesis that would be surgically implanted into Cassidy's leg bone. In a successful osseointegration procedure, the bone grows around the metal, holding it in place.

In the past, Marcellin-Little and Ola Harrysson, a professor in the NCSU Department of Industrial and Systems Engineering, had worked together to design and implant endoprostheses for cats. Harrysson incorporated the help of engineering graduate students to create the osseointegrated implants. The professors and students learned from every case, but Cassidy's procedure would be the first time the team ever performed osseointegration surgery on a larger animal.

There were dangers to the surgery, including the risks of infection or causing further damage to the leg bone. Harrysson and his students were testing designs that included an antibacterial coating on the endoprosthesis in the hopes that this coating would prevent infection.

The team took computed tomography, or CT, x-ray images of Cassidy's leg. Those CT images were used to create and print 3-D plastic models of Cassidy's residual limb. These models helped the team design the customized titanium endoprosthesis to be inserted into the bone.

During a four-hour surgery, Marcellin-Little placed the implant in Cassidy's leg bone and then stitched Cassidy's skin around the prostheses, leaving a small peg for the exoprosthesis to attach to.

Then Cassidy went home to rest and heal for about three months. This allowed time for the bone to grow around the metal and become strong enough to support an exoprosthesis. While Cassidy healed, the Posovskys cleaned the implant and Cassidy's skin multiple times each day with chlorhexidine, a strong disinfectant, to prevent infection.

In the meantime, Harrysson and his team took the x-rays, measurements, and other data they had gathered from Cassidy to continue their work. They created a leg and foot for Cassidy with sensors to measure the force generated when he walked, ran, and played. The data collected from the sensor would help them know how strong a final exoprosthesic foot needed to be.

In October 2008, Cassidy was fitted with this data-gathering exoprosthesis, lovingly called a "pogo stick" by Posovsky. Then the Posovskys took Cassidy home and began the work of teaching Cassidy to walk on four legs again. According to Posovsky, "He didn't know what a leg was. So I literally had to put one foot in front of the other." One day, while Posovsky was practicing with Cassidy, the hours of physical therapy began to pay off and Cassidy finally understood how to use his new leg. As Posovsky describes, "He just went, 'You know what? I can do this!' and he walked all on his own."

For Cassidy's permanent foot, the team created a carbon fiber frame with rubber treads that could be replaced as the rubber wore down. The foot attached to Cassidy's titanium endoprosthesis with a magnet. If the foot were to become tangled or trapped, the magnet would release and allow the prosthetic foot to detach from the rest of the leg. Harrysson and his students designed a C-shaped leg, similar to a human running prosthesis, because this type of leg would provide more bounce in Cassidy's step.

Eight months after his first surgery, Cassidy was fitted with his permanent foot. Soon after his endoprosthesis was attached, Cassidy walked up and down the halls of the College of Veterinary Medicine.

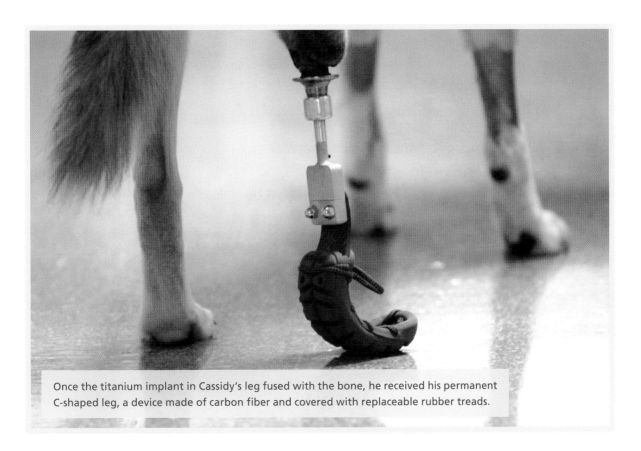

Once the titanium implant in Cassidy's leg fused with the bone, he received his permanent C-shaped leg, a device made of carbon fiber and covered with replaceable rubber treads.

Denis Marcellin-Little examines Cassidy's new leg while owner Stephen Posovsky offers his support.

Posovsky was overjoyed with Cassidy's new leg, and Cassidy seemed happy too! Posovsky reflected on the changes in Cassidy's life from the time he'd first seen the skinny, injured dog with patchy fur. "All of [a] sudden, he gets this beautiful coat of hair and a leg to walk on and run on the sand—I mean, literally RUN on the beach."

Transdermal osseointegrated prostheses remove issues of chafing and pain that can happen when donning prostheses with sockets. Osseointegrated prostheses also allow for more natural movement, which Cassidy took full advantage of. There are a few drawbacks, though, and surgeries like Cassidy's are helping researchers, surgeons, and engineers learn more and solve problems. According to Marcellin-Little, "These implants remain investigative because patients are vulnerable to infection at the interface between the skin and implant. Once that problem is solved, transdermal osseointegrated implants will likely revolutionize [this work]." He says, "We believe that this is the future of prosthetics."

With the Posovskys' support, Cassidy's surgery was successful and life-changing. Posovsky says, "In town, everyone who saw his leg would stop us and say, 'I've never seen anything like that before!' A surgery like this—it had never been done before. This was a labor of love."

OSSEOINTEGRATION EXPERIMENTATION: CASSIDY

Marcellin-Little and Harrysson had to consider the length that Cassidy's new leg should be as well as how the leg would move and function. Marcellin-Little also had to be very cautious while doing Cassidy's surgery because a broken bone or endoprosthesis could cause more problems for Cassidy. Create your own model of Cassidy's leg, and think about some of those same issues.

SUPPLIES NEEDED

- **marshmallows of varied sizes and/or a sticky candy like gumdrops or gummies (vegan if desired)**
- **uncooked spaghetti noodles**

1. Choose a large marshmallow or piece of candy to represent Cassidy's back hip.
2. Use an uncooked spaghetti noodle to represent the endoprosthesis.
3. Add a smaller marshmallow or piece of candy at the bottom of the noodle to represent Cassidy's exoprosthetic foot. What happens if you break your noodle leg in half and use a marshmallow or gummy candy in the middle to create a joint?
4. Now that you've made a leg prototype, experiment with it! Make new models. Try breaking your spaghetti pieces into different lengths. What happens when the noodle is long? What happens when the noodle is short? How does adding a second noodle of the same length beside the first noodle affect the leg? What happens to your marshmallow or candy when you've moved the spaghetti around too much? Has anything happened to the spaghetti too? How does that relate to Cassidy's body and the endoprosthesis? What other changes can you make to this endoprosthesis model that will allow for more movement and bending?

CHAPTER 4

VITÓRIA'S NEW BEAK

A Greylag Goose's Story

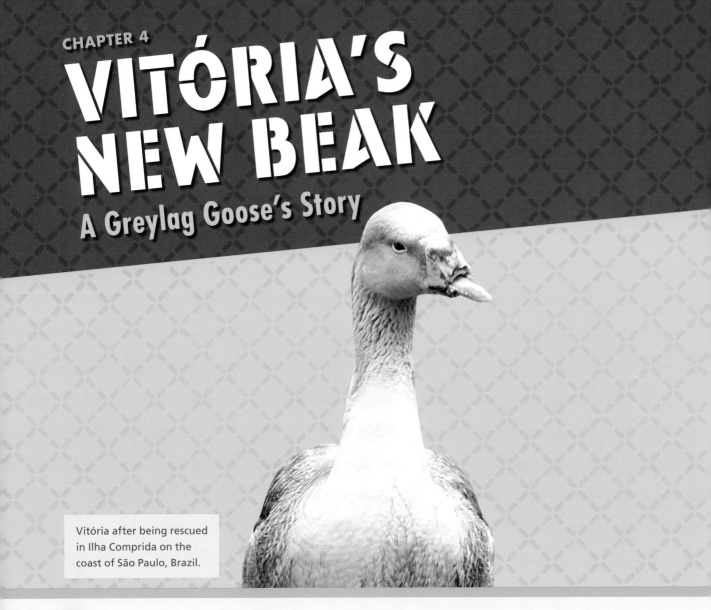

Vitória after being rescued in Ilha Comprida on the coast of São Paulo, Brazil.

In 2015, a greylag goose was found in Ilha Comprida, on the coast of São Paulo, Brazil. She was injured and had lost most of her beak. Rescuers thought she might have been attacked by dogs or hurt by humans. The goose was taken in by biologist and environmental technologist Cristian Negrão at Amigos do Mar, Friends of the Sea. Negrão named the goose Vitória, a Portuguese word that means "victory," something that everyone who met Vitória wanted for her.

This was the first time Amigos do Mar had helped a bird without a beak, though, and Vitória had lost a lot of weight because she wasn't able to eat the plants and grain that greylag geese normally eat. Vitória was also angry and aggressive. She didn't want people to touch her, but eventually she trusted Negrão enough to allow him to feed her baby food. Negrão knew he had to do something more to help Vitória, though, since her beak would never grow back and she was struggling to eat and drink.

Negrão reached out to the Unimonte Veterinary Hospital in Santos, Brazil, and a group of doctors and specialists calling themselves the Animal Avengers offered to help. The Animal Avengers team is made up of four veterinarians (Roberto Fecchio, Sergio Camargo, Matheus Rabello, and Rodrigo Rabello), a dental surgeon (Paulo Eduardo Miamoto Dias), and a 3-D designer (Cícero Moraes). Together, they've volunteered their expertise, time, and resources to create prostheses for numerous animals in Brazil.

The team realized that Vitória would die without their help. Miamoto and Fecchio made a mold of Vitória's injured beak area and noted that both the rhinotheca, or top beak, and the gnathotheca, or lower beak, were affected.

The Animal Avengers had also helped toucans, parrots, and a crow, but each of those birds only had their top or bottom beak damaged, not both. Vitória's case was unique and challenging because the team had to engineer a top and bottom beak that would fit properly and allow Vitória to eat and preen.

OTHER ANIMAL AVENGER RESCUES

Vitória wasn't the first creature assisted by the Animal Avengers. They've helped Freddy, a tortoise whose shell was burned in a brush fire; Hanna, a Labrador puppy who broke her canine tooth and couldn't eat properly; and numerous other birds, including toucans Bicolino, Tuc-Tuc, Zazu, Pirata, and Zequinha; parrots Gigi and Verdinho; and Giada the crow.

Being released in the wild won't be an option for the animals that the Animal Avengers have helped, so these animals are being cared for in sanctuaries because they may need new prostheses in the future.

Some of the animals' prostheses are printed in metal so they will be sturdy and strong, like Gigi's titanium beak and Hanna's chromium and cobalt incisor, while others, including Vitória's, are printed in polylactic plastic.

The team donates their time and resources to help these animals and has hired artists to paint some of the 3-D-printed beaks and Freddy's shell to make them look more realistic. They also share their 3-D-printing files online so others can learn from and utilize the work they've done.

How did these professionals get started helping animals? According to veterinarian Roberto Fecchio, they were all friends who loved both science and animals. Soon they realized they could work together, using their unique skills and innovative technologies to help design prostheses for animals in need.

The team used a technique called photogrammetry to design the new beak. The doctors compared photographs of the cast of Vitória's broken beak to photographs of similar greylag geese with intact beaks. They took measurements and made calculations to figure out the dimensions of the prosthesis.

Moraes used software to design Vitória's new beak as a 3-D model. Once the beak was created, Miamoto 3-D printed it in polylactic acid, or PLA. PLA plastic is a type of bioplastic created from products like sugarcane or corn starch and is more affordable than petroleum-based plastics. After being printed, the pieces of the beak were smoothed, polished, and painted with a yellow dental resin. The team was ready to attach Vitória's beak.

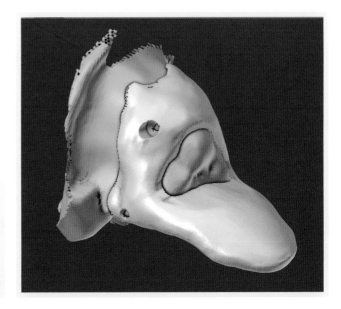

Vitória's surgery lasted nearly two hours. Her new beak was held in place with small screws. After almost fifty days without a beak, Vitória was finally able to eat and preen, or groom her feathers.

Right: This is the upper beak designed in Blender, a free 3-D software, by Cícero Moraes. The green portion shows what remains of Vitória's beak, and the white portion represents the 3-D-printed beak. *Bottom*: Vitória in the operating room after having her new 3-D beak printed and attached.

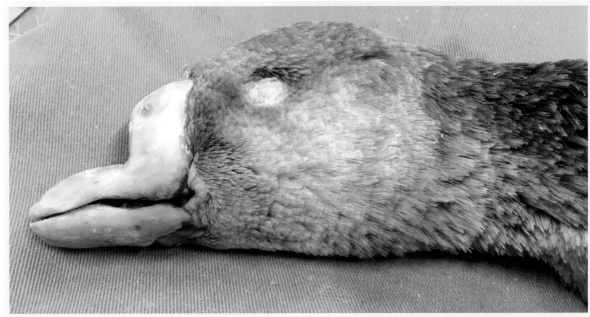

STUDENTS USING 3-D PRINTING TO HELP ANIMALS

With the guidance of teachers, students are also designing 3-D-printed prostheses for animals. In 2016 students from the Art Institute of Colorado created various iterations of a prosthesis to help Sonic, a kitten born without a bone in one of his front legs.

Tucker the Australian shepherd dog was born without bones in his back right foot, and his owner asked the 3-D printing club at the University of Missouri to make Tucker a prosthesis. Early prototypes were made of plastic and metal, but the students finally created Tucker's prosthesis entirely from PLA.

In San Juan Capistrano, California, a high school 3D Makerz club created a prosthetic leg for Isabelle, a chihuahua-terrier dog. Students took measurements and designed a prototype. The prosthesis didn't fit properly the first time, so students made adjustments.

In Amorel, Arkansas, eighth grade students helped create a prosthesis for Peg, a duck who lost his foot. The students went through over thirty iterations of PLA 3-D feet for Peg before finding a model that would allow his knee to bend and help him stay balanced while walking.

These students are helping prove that 3-D printing can change lives!

Sonic the kitten wears the new prosthetic paw that was custom designed for him by college students.

Vitória's beak lasted approximately four months before she began to have problems with it, and the Animal Avenger team stepped in to design a second-generation prosthesis. They decided that the first beak was too heavy and chose to create a more streamlined design—a beak that would be about one-third the size of the original prosthesis. In addition to photogrammetry, the team used x-rays and detailed anatomical studies to ensure the prosthesis would be an exact fit for Vitória.

Vitória with her mate Vitório and their two goslings at the Amigos do Mar sanctuary

GREYLAG GEESE

Greylag geese are found worldwide, with large concentrations in Europe. The majority of greylag populations are domesticated, and evidence exists that greylags were the geese domesticated by the ancient Egyptians around three thousand years ago. Greylags typically live near water and might be found around marshes, lakes, and coasts. They range from white to gray in coloring. On average, they are 30 to 32 inches (76 to 81 cm) long and weigh 6.4 to 8.2 pounds (2.9 to 3.7 kg). These large, strong geese have muscular necks and will fight to defend their eggs and babies.

Moraes said, "This prosthesis, besides being smaller, is lighter and more elegant. To get to this stage was a lengthy process. It was our most difficult surgery, but undoubtedly a very educational and groundbreaking one." During this process, the Animal Avengers explored new technologies and proved to the world that a bird without a beak can be helped.

Negrão was overjoyed that the team had helped the bird he rescued. He said, "Vitória will have a new chance to survive and return to a normal life. She can become the first goose in the world to lose a beak and be completely rehabilitated."

Vitória has proven Negrão right. She met a mate, Vitório, at the Amigos do Mar sanctuary, and in 2016 she became the mother to two goslings. Using her prosthetic beak, she was able to feed, bathe, and groom her babies.

BUILD-A-BEAK: VITÓRIA

Build a paper beak so you can explore the ways birds use their beaks. Then modify the beak to experience some of the challenges Vitória might have dealt with after her injury.

SUPPLIES NEEDED

- **2 or 3 pieces of paper—cardstock or thinner paper**
- **ruler**
- **scissors**
- **glue stick or tape**

1. Start with square pieces of paper—for example, 6 inches (15 cm) long by 6 inches wide—OR measure and cut 2 pieces of paper to a square size.
2. Fold one of the papers in half diagonally. This diagonal line will be your centerline. Fold the right lower edge to the centerline. Fold the left lower edge to the centerline. Overlap the flat part of the folds, and then glue or tape them together. This is one-half of your beak.
3. Repeat the same steps on the other piece of paper to make the other half of the beak.
4. Cut a strip of paper, and glue or tape the strip between the two open ends of the beak to hold it together.
5. Use your beak by inserting your fingers in one side and your thumb in the other side—or observe a friend using the beak.
6. Test the beak! Can you pick up small rocks or seeds? Try preening feathers if you have some available, or groom your own hair (be careful not to poke yourself). How would your beak be affected if the point of it were gone? If you were a bird and your beak were injured or broken, how might searching for food or cleaning yourself be changed?

CHAPTER 5
PIRATE'S MODIFIED LEG
A Berkshire-Tamworth Pig's Story

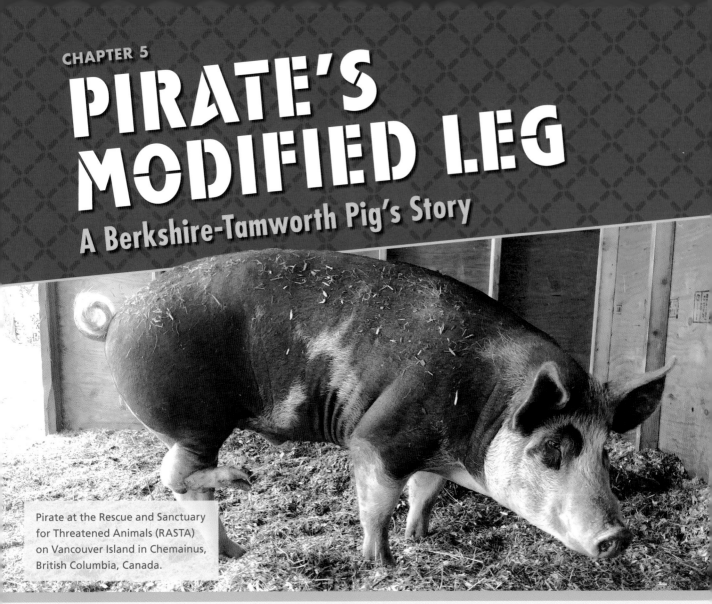

Pirate at the Rescue and Sanctuary for Threatened Animals (RASTA) on Vancouver Island in Chemainus, British Columbia, Canada.

Two piglets were born in western Canada in the spring of 2016. The owner of the farm where they'd been born planned to sell them as "BBQ piglets," baby pigs that would be cooked and eaten. But even though they were being raised for their meat, the piglets were neglected and slowly starving.

In August 2016, the malnourished piglets were discovered and taken in by the Rescue and Sanctuary for Threatened Animals (RASTA) on Vancouver Island in Chemainus, British Columbia, Canada. Both piglets were hungry and scared. They were covered in lice and infested with intestinal worms. RASTA staff nurtured them, naming the little black-and-white pig Pirate (because of the patchlike spot over one eye) and his orange-and-black brother Prince.

RASTA founder, Lucie Cerny, noticed Pirate's back leg as soon as she saw him and wondered if the leg had been broken. The piglets were neglected at their old home, so an untreated injury like that was possible. However, after consulting numerous veterinarians, Cerny learned that Pirate was likely born with a fused tarsal joint in his hock, midway up his leg. The little pig's right hind leg was permanently bent forward at a 90-degree angle, and he couldn't move the joint. The remainder of Pirate's leg was twisted and weak. After examinations and x-rays, specialists said surgery wouldn't help Pirate walk again.

Cerny watched Pirate. He was able to hobble or drag himself along, but he twisted his spine to avoid putting weight on his bent hock. Most of Cerny's rescue pigs at RASTA are potbellied pigs, but Pirate and his brother Prince are Berkshire-Tamworth pigs, and Lucie knew Pirate might weigh 700 pounds (318 kg) or more once he was fully grown.

Pirate (*left*) and his brother Prince were rescued when they were just a few months old.

BERKSHIRE AND TAMWORTH PIGS

Both Berkshire and Tamworth pigs originated in the United Kingdom, but there are distinct differences between the two breeds.

Tamworth pigs are said to be a cross between wild English boars and Irish pigs. Tamworths have long bodies and are strong and athletic. This breed foraged for meals in the forests of England, using their strong snouts to root out food like acorns in the leaves of the forest floor. Tamworth pigs often have red coats, powerful legs, and are extremely smart.

Berkshire pigs are one of the oldest English breeds. They are generally black with small white areas on their nose, feet, and tails. Berkshires have short legs and do well finding food outside, but they don't usually roam the long distances like Tamworths do because of their shorter legs. Female Berkshires are known to be good mothers. This breed is usually friendly, often curious, and very smart.

Pirate is a Berkshire-Tamworth pig. This means he has ancestors from the Berkshire breed of pigs and ancestors from the Tamworth breed, and he represents the best of both breeds!

According to Cerny, "Unlike lighter and more agile animals like dogs and cats, pigs don't usually do well with three legs because of their tremendous weight and the challenges of their anatomy with having such long backs." Being able to use only three of his four legs was going to cause Pirate pain and shorten his life.

Cerny met with more veterinarians, asking what could be done to help Pirate. Susan Calverley reviewed Pirate's case. When she looked at his x-rays and watched videos of the little pig moving, she was confident that an orthosis (a device such as a brace) or prosthesis would help Pirate. Pirate's limb difference meant he needed a hybrid orthosis-prosthesis to support his leg and add length so he could stand and move normally.

Cerny began the work of finding the proper device for Pirate and raising funds to pay for it. Because Pirate was just a piglet, he would likely need four to five different devices as he grew, and most orthoses cost thousands of dollars. Luckily, the vegan restaurant Café la Vie offered to help sponsor Pirate. After a few attempts to find someone who could design a brace, orthotist Tim Witoski at Island Orthotics in Victoria volunteered his services and time, driving over an hour each way to meet with Pirate. Witoski usually works with humans and dogs to create custom orthoses, but he was happy to use his knowledge and experience to help the pig.

Witoski worked with Pirate to help create an orthosis-prosthesis that would allow the pig to move around the RASTA grounds. The goal in designing a device for Pirate was to craft something that could support his bent leg and provide the needed length that would allow Pirate to distribute his weight more evenly to all four legs.

Above: Pirate testing one of Tim Witoski's early designs. This device featured a prosthetic human foot that Witoski modified. *Right*: Tim Witoski, from Island Orthotics, works on an updated version of Pirate's device.

Witoski experimented with parts. One brace he created featured recycled parts, including a base shaped like a human foot that had been modified to help Pirate balance. The newest model, though, is made of sturdy plastic that is strong enough to support hundreds of pounds of weight but lightweight enough that Pirate can run and play all day while wearing it.

To create Pirate's brace, Witoski made a cast mold of Pirate's shortened left hind limb using fiberglass casting material, the same material used in casting broken arms or legs in humans. Witoski filled this cast, also called a negative mold, with plaster. This plaster, basically a copy of Pirate's leg, is a positive mold. Witoski vacuum-formed layers of heat-moldable foam over the positive mold. A firm, liquid foam compound created the limb extension below the foam layers. Witoski took measurements from Pirate's shortened leg to the ground, and the foam compound was shaped until the extension would be the same length as Pirate's other back leg.

WOODSTOCK FARM SANCTUARY

Woodstock Farm Sanctuary in New York is similar to RASTA. It provides a home for neglected, abused, or abandoned farm animals. Animals at Woodstock who have needed prostheses include Felix the sheep. When Felix was a baby, he was attacked by a predator and lost his rear left leg. Jenny Brown, cofounder and executive director of Woodstock Farm Sanctuary, wanted to help. She spoke to the prosthetist who made her own prosthetic leg, Erik Tomkins, to see if he would be willing to design a leg for Felix (*pictured below*). Tomkins used what he knows about human prostheses and reached out to students at the Hudson Valley Advanced Manufacturing Center in the State University of New York (SUNY) at New Paltz so they could help design and 3-D print a leg for Felix.

Woodstock is also home to Albie, a goat who has tried a prosthetic leg and wheels to support his walking, and Fawn, a cow who has braces on her front legs.

Pirate wearing a Witoski-designed orthotic device that rocks as he walks, allowing him to balance and keep up with his friends at RASTA

After Witoski had the shape of the orthosis, he moved on to the plastic molding stage. Witoski heated a sheet of polypropylene plastic in an oven until the hard plastic became pliable— "similar in consistency to a cooked lasagna noodle," according to Witoski. The soft plastic was wrapped around the foam skeleton of the orthosis. Once the plastic hardened, Witoski cut it from the cast and sanded and smoothed all the edges. He attached Velcro straps to secure the orthosis to Pirate's leg and added a base layer of rubber to the gently curved bottom that would allow Pirate to move across the grounds of RASTA.

As of November 2019, Pirate weighs over 500 pounds (227 kg) and is wearing his fourth device. Each morning while Pirate eats his breakfast, Cerny straps the leg brace on. Before he had his brace, Pirate struggled to move and lost his balance easily. When he would lie down to cool himself and protect his skin by wallowing in mud, he had a difficult time getting up out of the wallow.

Now, though, Witoski says, "Since Pirate has been fitted with his custom-made orthosis, he's able to balance very well and is able to keep up with his buddy Prince when they wallow and play at the sanctuary."

WALK LIKE A PIG!

Humans walk on the bottoms of their feet, but most four-legged animals walk on their toes! Let's experiment with how an animal like a pig walks.

1. Find a space with a carpeted or padded floor.
2. If you are able, get down on your hands and feet and then balance yourself on the tips of your toes and fingers, or ask a friend to try this while you observe.
3. Try to move forward.
4. To understand how Pirate feels when he tries to walk without an orthosis, bend your left ankle up and try to walk with just your fingertips and your right toes.

How are you moving? Are you hopping? Wobbling? Did you fall? How would your movement be changed if you weighed hundreds of pounds as Pirate does? Think about large animals like Pirate the pig and Mosha the elephant. For them, having a limb difference causes a lot of stress on their remaining legs. How might this be different for a lighter, smaller animal like a fox or a deer? How might it impact an animal if the leg that is affected is a front leg? What might change if the leg that is affected is a back leg?

CONCLUSION

WHERE WOULD LOLA BE WITHOUT HER FLIPPER? Would Mosha, Cassidy, or Pirate be able to walk, play, and explore their environments without their prostheses? Would Vitória be able to feed herself and care for her babies if she didn't have a new beak? Around the world, people are thinking creatively and using innovative technologies to attempt to change animals' lives for the better.

People who help animals often work in partnership with other professionals. Surgeons, prosthetists, orthotists, 3-D designers, students, and others may share information that will help animals and humans. As new animal prostheses are created and designed, innovations will continue to occur. Animal prostheses will increasingly feature lightweight, strong materials, 3-D-printed elements, electronic parts that allow for more natural movement, and osseointegrated components.

When creating prostheses, designers use science, math, art, and engineering skills to take measurements, sketch and design various iterations, and create the final product. The creators also need patience, as the first design for a prosthesis is usually not the final design! People who make prostheses for animals often need to modify their prototypes and adapt designs based on how the animal responds and how the prosthesis functions. Through their hard work and persistence, though, people of all ages and with various educational backgrounds are changing animals' lives. Will you join them? How might you help animals?

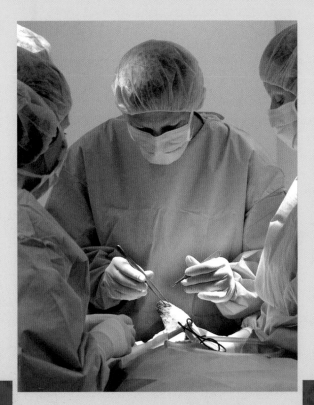

Denis Marcellin-Little prepares to implant an endoprosthesis in Cassidy's leg at the North Carolina State University College of Veterinary Medicine in Raleigh, North Carolina.

Mosha's mahout, Palahdee Sujaritsuchada, puts on Mosha's prosthetic leg at the Friends of the Asian Elephant Hospital in Lampang, Thailand.

Therdchai Jivacate sketches a new prosthetic leg for Mosha at his Chiang Mai University Prosthetics Lab in Chiang Mai, Thailand.

GLOSSARY

amputation: the removal of part or all of a body part

amputee: a person or animal who is born with a limb difference or who has lost part or all of a limb through surgery, accident, or injury

biomimetic: something that imitates nature

bionic: artificial body parts that help an animal or human to function or move

bioplastic: a type of plastic that is made from natural, biodegradable, renewable sources such as wood chips or vegetable oils rather than petroleum products

carbon fiber: a strong, lightweight fiber that is created by twisting together many thin strands of carbon. It is also known as graphite fiber.

computed tomography: a type of scan that uses computer processing of x-rays taken at different angles to create images of what the inside of a person or animal looks like. It is also known as a CT scan.

endoprostheses: a prosthesis that is placed inside a person or animal's body, generally through osseointegration

exoprosthesis: a prosthesis that is used outside the body, generally attaching to an osseointegrated endoprosthesis

iteration: repeating something or making something again, usually in the hopes of improving it

limb difference: having limbs that are different in some way. Limb difference can be congenital, meaning the person or animal is born that way, or limb difference can be acquired, meaning the person or animal's limb difference happens after birth

natal homing: the practice of creatures returning to the place where they hatched or were born, such as sea turtles returning to the same beach where they hatched. Scientists hypothesize that turtles use Earth's magnetic fields and a heightened sense of smell to accomplish this.

orthopedist: a doctor who specializes in correcting bone injuries and issues. Also known as an orthopedic surgeon.

orthosis: (plural: orthoses) a brace or device that helps support a part of the body. From the Greek word *orthosis*, meaning "straightening."

orthotics: the science of creating orthoses

orthotist: a person who designs and fits orthoses

osseointegration: placing a prosthesis into or around the bone, such as Cassidy's endoprosthesis. The root word is the Latin word *osseus*, which means "bone." It is also known as osteointegration, or transdermal osseointegration.

photogrammetry: using art, science, and technology, photogrammetry makes measurements from photographs in order to create a 3-D model, map, drawing, etc. The prefix *photo-* means "picture," and the root *-grammetry means* "measurement."

plastic forming: a way to shape plastic that is used in creating prostheses. Plastic can be shaped by thermoforming, or heating it. Heated plastic can be shaped when a vacuum is used to remove the air from a mold, also known as vacuum forming, or when a 3-D mold is pressed against warm, pliable plastic, known as pressure forming.

prosthesis: (plural: prostheses) an artificial limb or body part, from the Greek word *prosthetikós*, meaning "giving added power"

prosthetics: the science of creating prostheses. The word *prosthetic* can also be used as an adjective to describe something, like a prosthetic flipper or prosthetic sock.

prosthetist: a person who designs and fits prostheses

prototype: the first iteration of something. The Greek root *proto-* means "first formed."

residual limb: after an amputation or loss of a limb, the residual limb is the part of the body remaining

socket: the part of a prosthesis that fits around a residual limb

titanium: a very light, strong, durable silver-colored metal

transdermal: Below the skin. The prefix *trans-* means "through" or "under," and the root *-derm* means "skin."

SOURCE NOTES

10 "Students Create First-of-Its Kind Prosthetic Flipper for Maimed Sea Turtle," Worcester Polytechnic Institute, September 16, 2016, https://www.wpi.edu/news/students-create-first-its-kind-prosthetic-flipper-maimed-sea-turtle; "WPI Students Create Prosthetic Flipper for Maimed Sea Turtle," YouTube video, 1:43, posted by WPI, September 14, 2016, https://www.youtube.com/watch?v=qXS2BgAu814&feature=youtu.be.

11 Vivian Liang, Samantha Varela, and Iok Wong, "Design of a Flipper Prosthetic for a Kemp's Ridley Sea Turtle," WPI, accessed May 18, 2019, https://web.wpi.edu/Pubs/E-project/Available/E-project-042816-150116/unrestricted/Sea_Turtle_MQP_FINAL_REPORT.pdf; Samantha Varela, email message to the author, May 16, 2019.

11 Samantha Varela, email message to the author, September 9, 2018.

11 Kevin Carroll, "Lola and Rocky took to their new flippers in no time!," Facebook, September 23, 2018, https://www.facebook.com/watch/?v=1910369862603227.

12 Genya Yerkes, telephone conversation with author, March 14, 2019.

12 Varela, email, September 9, 2018.

12 "Students Create Flipper," Worcester Polytechnic Institute.

15 The Eyes of Thailand, directed by Windy Borman (Murrieta, CA: FilmWorks Entertainment, 2012), DVD.

17–18 "One Step at a Time: The First Elephant Prosthetics," YouTube video, 2:35, posted by Great Big Story, June 14, 2016, https://www.youtube.com/watch?v=Yyp4alF7iL0.

18 "One Step at a Time."

21 Stephen Posovsky, telephone conversation with author, May 20, 2019.

21 Susan Posovsky, telephone conversation with author, May 20, 2019.

23 Stephen Posovsky, telephone conversation with author, April 23, 2019.

24 Posovsky.

24 Denis Marcellin-Little, email message to author, May 15, 2019.

24 Tracey Peake, "Groundbreaking Surgical Procedure Will Allow Dog with Amputated Limb to Walk on Four Legs Again," NC State University, accessed May 18, 2019, https://news.ncsu.edu/2008/07/groundbreaking-surgical-procedure-will-allow-dog-with-amputated-limb-to-walk-on-four-legs-again/.

24 Stephen Posovsky, telephone conversation, May 20, 2019.

30 Luna Oliva, "Gansa ganha bico impresso em 3D e se reabilita após procedimento inédito," globo.com, July 7, 2016, http://g1.globo.com/sp/santos-regiao/noticia/2016/07/gansa-ganha-bico-impresso-em-3d-e-se-reabilita-apos-procedimento-inedito.html.

30 "Após quase ser sacrificada, gansa que ganhou bico artificial vira mãe em SP," globo.com, August 11, 2016, http://g1.globo.com/sp/santos-regiao/noticia/2016/11/apos-quase-ser-sacrificada-gansa-que-ganhou-bico-artificial-vira-mae-em-sp.html.

34 RASTA Sanctuary, "When we rescued Pirate," Facebook, July 18, 2018, https://www.facebook.com/RastaRescue/photos/a.630636176957413/1920587497962268/?type=3&theater.

36 Tim Witoski, email message to author, May 24, 2019.

36 Witoski.

SELECTED BIBLIOGRAPHY

LOLA

Amos, Tony. "One Turtle's Amazing Odyssey." *Port Aransas South Jetty*, October 27, 2016. https://www.portasouthjetty.com/articles/one-turtles-amazing-odyssey/.

Liang, Vivian, Samantha Varela, and Iok Wong. "Design of a Flipper Prosthetic for a Kemp's Ridley Sea Turtle." WPI, Accessed November 11, 2019. https://web.wpi.edu/Pubs/E-project /Available/E-project-042816-150116/unrestricted/Sea_Turtle_MQP_FINAL_REPORT.pdf.

MOSHA

Paddock, Richard C. "Mosha, Thai Elephant Wounded by Land Mine, Gets New Prosthetic Limb." *NY Times*, July 1, 2016. https://www.nytimes.com/2016/07/02/world/asia/thailand-elephant -prosthetic-leg.html.

CASSIDY

"Medical Pioneer Cassidy Receives Final Prosthetic Limb." NC State, March 31, 2008. https://cvm .ncsu.edu/medical-pioneer-cassidy-receives-final-prosthetic-limb/.

VITÓRIA

Arnold, Carrie. "Injured Animals Get Second Chance with 3-D Printed Limbs." *National Geographic*, August 19, 2016. https://www.nationalgeographic.com/news/2016/08 /prosthetics-animals-rescued-3d-dogs-cats/.

PIRATE

"Sawatsky Sign-Off: Pirate the Pig." CTV News, December 15, 2018. https://vancouverisland .ctvnews.ca/video?clipId=1565784&fbclid=IwAR019SUq5K7k-mgCFLYHG067rzvrQ8nWJ1Nws8A sxqIshoylcXWcjrCEla4.

LEARN MORE

Key West Aquarium
https://www.keywestaquarium.com/
The Key West Aquarium is home to Lola, Rocky, and many sharks, fish, and other creatures. The aquarium also teaches visitors about conservation and preservation of the Florida Keys ecosystem, which includes many endangered species and houses the only living barrier reef system in North America.

Friends of the Asian Elephant Hospital
http://www.friendsoftheasianelephant.org/en/
Soraida Salwala has dedicated her life to elephants and created the Friends of the Asian Elephant Hospital. Salwala and volunteers like Jivacate have helped thousands of elephants at the elephant hospital, and Salwala has fought for the rights of Thai elephants and promoted conservation for decades.

Redland Rock Pit Abandoned Dogs Project
https://www.redlandrockpit.org/
Stephen and Susan Posovsky's favorite dog rescue is the Redland Rock Pit Abandoned Dogs Project. Southwestern Dade County in Florida is known as a dog dumping ground, a place where thousands of dogs have been abandoned by their owners. The Posovskys support the Redland Rock Pit Abandoned Dogs Project by volunteering their time, donating resources, and adopting special needs and senior animals.

Rescue and Sanctuary for Threatened Animals (RASTA)
http://rastarescue.org/
Lucie Cerny founded the Rescue and Sanctuary for Threatened Animals (RASTA). RASTA provides a safe place for abandoned and abused animals for the rest of their lives, and Cerny and her organization educate people and advocate for animal rights. RASTA also partners with local vegan restaurants to teach their community that veganism helps end animal suffering.

NUBTribe
https://www.nubtribe.com/
Sensitivity readers Karen, Mike, and Selah Gilbert founded NUBTribe. NUBTribe provides information about limb difference and support to individuals with limb differences.

INDEX

ACKNOWLEDGMENTS

With gratitude to my family and writing friends for listening to rough drafts, testing out activities, and giving me snacks and space so I could work.

Carol Hinz, this book would never have existed without your saying yes, and instead of just plain yes, you said, "Yes, and what might happen if you added more information?" and "Yes, and what might happen if we added activities?" You asked thoughtful questions that encouraged me to push myself and this manuscript to make it the best it could be. Thank you. I'm so grateful you were my guide on this journey!

For helping create the most beautiful, factual, and kid-friendly book possible, my thanks to everyone at Millbrook Press.

A very special thanks to Karen, Mike, and Selah Gilbert from NUBTribe for taking the time to read and discuss *Bionic Beasts* with me! Your willingness to share your experiences and knowledge has helped make this book inclusive and informational. I thank you and the readers thank you.

Samantha Varela and Genya Yerkes, thank you for the messages, emails, and phone conversations about Lola. I'm in awe of the work you and your team did, Samantha. And Genya, I'm in awe of the work your aquarium does daily.

Soraida Salwala, you have shown me what the strength and conviction of one person can do. Thank you for this and for answering my endless questions about Mosha. You are changing the world, one elephant at a time.

Stephen and Susan Posovsky, your love of animals is evident. Thank you for taking the time to talk with me about Cassidy and your family's journey, and thank you for being willing to save lives. Dr. Denis Marcellin-Little, thank you for helping me to better understand the intricacies of the groundbreaking surgeries you perform.

Cícero Moraes, thank you for sharing your design work with the world, helping animals in need, and for talking with me about your team and Vitória.

Lucie Cerny, thank you for being a fierce advocate for animals. Pirate and all the animals at RASTA Sanctuary are fortunate to have found you. Tim Witoski, thank you for supporting Pirate, and much gratitude for the great activity idea in Pirate's chapter—we expanded that idea throughout the book!

PHOTO ACKNOWLEDGMENTS

Image credits: Cicero Moraes/Wikimedia Commons (CC BY-SA 4.0), pp. 2, 26, 28, 30; Richard Whitcombe/Shutterstock.com, p. 6; Monty Rakusen/Cultura/Getty Images, p. 7; Key West Aquarium, pp. 8, 12; Michael Patrick O'Neill/Alamy Stock Photo, p. 9 (top); Paulo Oliveira/Alamy Stock Photo, p. 9 (bottom); Rob O'Neal for Worcester Polytechnic Institute, p. 10; Bronek Kaminski/Barcroft Media/Getty Images, pp. 14, 18; Jungle Man/500px Prime/Getty Images, p. 15; Peter Charlesworth/LightRocket/Getty Images, p. 16; Taylor Weidman/LightRocket/Getty Images, pp. 17, 39; Jolene Gutiérrez, pp. 19, 31; Steve Posovsky, pp. 20, 21; Corey Lowenstein/Raleigh News & Observer/Tribune News Service/Getty Images, pp. 22, 38; AP Photo/The News & Observer, Shawn Rocco, pp. 23, 24; Andy Cross/The Denver Post/Getty Images, p. 29; RASTA Sanctuary, pp. 32, 33, 34 (right), 36; Tim Witoski, p. 34 (left); Adrienne Gallagher, p. 35.

Cover Images: Bronek Kaminski/Barcroft Media/Getty Images.